Masterful Publishing
PO Box 6248
McKinney, Texas 75070
angela@masterfulcollective.com
www.angelaandamaya.com

❧

I thank God for the inspiration of the Holy Spirit which allowed me to write this booklet.

I DEDICATE THIS TO WIDOWS

To my parents,
Your love and inspiration is unmatched.

To my future husband, my other whole,
Your love creates momentum in my life.

To my daughter,
I was ordained to be your mother.
You are my greatest gift from God.

To my amazing siblings,
I can't imagine life without your support.

To my sisters in Christ,
You know the true meaning of friendship.

❧

CONTENTS

A NOTE FROM ANGELA

We moved as a family to Texas with a 9-month old sweet baby girl. She was our inspiration. We created several plans, one was to sit in rocking chairs on our porch watching our grandchildren play in the yard in our latter years.

Death summoned my spouse with unfinished plans and a long to-do list. Our daughter was 7 years old at the time. Wake me up from this terrible dream, how will I tell her? How will I go on without him? Time continued to move forward. It was at that time I could stop and take a deep breath. Life's circumstance forced me to be still. It was a blessing to be surrounded by an amazing support system and religious community. It was my choice to take one second of every minute of each hour to continue to live.

I created this journal to help other widows like myself. Like a tender friend, this open-ended journal asks honest and thoughtful questions you can work through at your own pace. So, I want to partner with you so you won't walk alone.

God left His peace for you. Let's grow together!

Blessings, Angela

Choosing to Live
After Losing a Spouse

"The Lord watches over the foreigner and sustains the fatherless and the widow, but he frustrates the ways of the wicked."

Psalm 146:9

Losing a Loved One

The air left the room at 3:43 a.m. on May 10, 2014. I awakened suddenly with a gasp, in a panic, looking around the room. Our daughter lay beside me, sound asleep. I believe it is at that time the Lord's Angel whispered your name; because we are one in flesh, I felt your spirit leave my body.

The death of a loved one creates an immediate emotional tornado that spins and spins and spins. They say every tornado has an eye, a place of inception and landing. As one who is grieving, where does anything begin or end when a vital person instantly becomes absent in your life? Feeling paralyzed, as if in a dream, I prayed to wake up to reality; I prayed, when will the nightmare end? Grief caused me to feel as if there was a wall keeping me from awareness of my current state. It was constantly forcing my mind to yesterday when my spouse was alive.

Grief is a normal and natural response that follows the death of a loved one. Grief is not an identity to be ashamed of; it is a journey to live. It's healthy to live the journey with forward momentum; it is not a destination with an end. It is not a linear timeline.

There are five primary steps of grief that allow those who are grieving to better understand what they are faced with. The stages of grief can come rushing in at the same time or one at a time and in no particular order. Over time, some of the feelings will intensify and their frequency will diminish, but in most instances you will experience each stage: denial, anger, bargaining, depression, and acceptance. Some expressions of grief may include shock, loneliness, confusion, guilt, and anger.

Reflection

Search your heart as you reflect on the questions.

- ❑ Emotionally, what are you thinking? What are the meditations of your mind?
- ❑ Physically, are you neglecting your physical needs for survival?
- ❑ Relationally, how are you interacting with those closest to you? Are you isolating yourself?
- ❑ Spiritually, how are you staying connected to the one true source of comfort and peace? Has your faith been questioned?

Describe the expressions of grief you have experienced.

_____

_____

_____

_____

_____

Describe the stages of grief you have experienced.

_____

_____

_____

_____

_____

Describe the expressions and feelings you don't understand.

_____

_____

_____

_____

_____

Understanding Grief

❦

Grief leaves a unique mark on each widow as her number is called. Every widow grieves in her own way and may experience several kinds of grief. A few types are listed below:

- ❑ **Anticipated grief.** This type is often experienced because you know what is about to happen. Your mind has accepted what is inevitable. You have a glimpse into what's next.

- ❑ **Unresolved grief.** This can occur when there are issues that are unresolved, and the layers of a new loss compound the situation.

- ❑ **Complicated grief.** This occurs when there is a sudden or traumatic death that was unexpected. This can include a murder, accident, or suicide.

Acceptance

It may be difficult to get to a place of acceptance, but it becomes a choice to live in the reality that your loved one will not be walking through the door again. He will never leave another voicemail. Acceptance doesn't mean everything is perfect, rather it is a recognition of your new, permanent reality. With this acceptance, you will still experience periods of emotional highs and lows.

❧❦

Reflection

Search your heart as you reflect on the questions.

How can you accept in faith that your loved one has departed from this life?

_____

_____

_____

_____

_____

_____

Describe physical signs that support your reply.

_____

_____

_____

_____

_____

_____

_____

Describe spiritual signs or scriptures that support your reply.

_____

_____

_____

_____

_____

_____

_____

_____

Release Your Emotions

It is important to release what you are feeling through conversation. Identify a trusted person to whom you can express any emotion. Two of the greatest emotions you may feel are anger and pain.

Anger can be directed toward your loved one due to feeling like they left you behind. You may be angry thinking of all of the unfinished plans you had together. Anger can be ignited when you begin to assess your current reality. You may have been left with a pile of household bills, minimal or no life insurance because the premium lapsed, or lack of forgiveness or closure for marital issues. Also, anger can be directed toward God who gives life and death. You may ask God why you have to endure such pain and heartbreak.

Peeling back the layer of anger, there is pain. The pain of separation from a source of love and companionship can feel piercing and unbearable. When those feelings seem too difficult to bear, call your trusted confidant or your religious leader. It is in those times of vulnerability that your thoughts can't be trusted. Satan will attempt to plant doubt and hopelessness in your mind. Feelings are fleeting, but God's word is a constant assurance of hope.

Reflection

Search your heart as you reflect on the questions.

What are some plans you can still accomplish without your loved one?

_____

_____

_____

_____

_____

_____

As you heal and regain strength daily, there are some temptations that you can experience related to grief. When we are most vulnerable, Satan will tempt us just as he tempted Jesus after His fast in the wilderness. See Matthew 4.

✤✤

Reflection

Search your heart as you reflect on the questions.

══════════════════════════════

Which of these temptations have you experienced? Add to the list as you see necessary.

- ❑ To give up
- ❑ To get in your car and drive until you run out of gas
- ❑ To hide from life
- ❑ To stay in the bed
- ❑ To fear going to sleep
- ❑ To quit your job

- ❑ To isolate yourself as if no one understands
- ❑ To envy others whose families are still together
- ❑ To overwork and overcommit
- ❑ To blame yourself
- ❑ To blame God
- ❑ To take drugs
- ❑ To overtake prescription medication
- ❑ To drink irresponsibly
- ❑ To overeat
- ❑ To become sexually promiscuous
- ❑ _____
- ❑ _____
- ❑ _____
- ❑ _____

Take a moment to journal your thoughts about any of the above experiences.

_____

_____

_____

_____

_____

_____

Surviving Loss

❧

*"Now may the Lord of Peace Himself give you peace
at all times and in every way. The Lord be with all of you."*

2 Thessalonians 3:16

Store Memories

Flood your mind with laughter by recalling moments you shared and stories of how you met, pulling out photographs, and celebrating the life they lived. It's funny how the little things we sometimes nagged about become vague, distant memories when our loved one is gone.

Share a precious memory that you and your loved one experienced together. Don't leave out all of the smiles and emotions that come along with the memory. Consider sharing about the life they lived with someone you trust. Tell your children a wedding blunder or a funny story that happened when you were dating. We know men and women have different perspectives on who pursued whom!

The Domino Effect

Losing a husband is both physical and relational. He is no longer physically present, but there are also roles he will no longer fill. They are intangible layers of loss, such as being the breadwinner, the mechanic, the partner, the lover, the protector, the handyman, and the friend. All of this disappears in an instant. You will have to separate yourself out of your couple identity.

You may discover new losses each day. Be honest with your feelings. The following reflection shows a short list. Please use this only as a guide, as you may have more losses to add to the list.

Reflection

Search your heart as you reflect on the questions.

Check all that apply (add to the list as necessary):

- ❑ Financial Provider

- ❑ Companion

- ❑ Confidant

- ❑ Lover

- ❑ Encourager

- ❑ Cook

- ❑ Mechanic

- ❑ Gardener
- ❑ Best Friend
- ❑ Protector
- ❑ Leader
- ❑ Adventure Partner
- ❑ Computer Repairman
- ❑ Handyman
- ❑ Driver
- ❑ Massage Therapist
- ❑ Movie Date
- ❑ _____
- ❑ _____
- ❑ _____
- ❑ _____
- ❑ _____
- ❑ _____
- ❑ _____

Take a moment to journal about an area(s) of concern from the list above, and plan how you will compensate for the loss(es).

_____

_____

_____

_____

_____

_____

_____

_____

_____

_____

_____

_____

_____

_____

_____

_____

_____

Reinvest in Life

Time doesn't stop when we lose a spouse, so we cannot stop. Look around you. Life is still moving on. People are having celebrations; wedding plans are in the works; some are experiencing promotions in their job; your children may be in sports and outside activities. Make a conscious effort each and every day to continue to live. This choice will keep you from becoming stuck in grief or trapped in time.

Accepting feelings of grief in everyday life, while not drowning in sorrow, is an effective and great way to take small steps forward.

Reflection

Search your heart as you reflect on the questions.

Realize your new identity is permanent. Discover the new "you." Who are you now?

_____

_____

_____

_____

_____

What new responsibilities will you have to embrace?

_____

_____

_____

_____

_____

What new losses have you experienced?

_____

_____

_____

_____

_____

Grief Resembles Abandonment

If you have any unresolved parental issues, those can resurface. Also, if your friend circles include primarily couples, that may change. You will be the odd person out, so you may not be invited to couples' outings. You may feel abandoned by groups in your community. If this occurs, re-establish yourself by finding a new community of support and social activity.

Find comfort in accepting the pain of your past. The revived feelings of abandonment need to be compartmentalized so that you do not become trapped in regret and grief. Accept the pain of your childhood; accept the pain of your current loss, and build from that place.

Reflection

Search your heart as you reflect on the questions.

Is there someone that abandoned you that needs your forgiveness?

_____

_____

_____

_____

_____

Describe what you'd like your healing journey to look like.

_____

_____

_____

_____

_____

According to 2 Thessalonians 3:16, how have you experienced God's peace?

_____

_____

_____

_____

_____

Giving to others can sometimes help to alleviate pain. Have you lost your ability to give to others? If so, are you experiencing self-pity? Explain your feelings.

_____

_____

_____

_____

_____

Name five things for which you are thankful.

_____

_____

_____

_____

_____

Rushed Grief

Our culture is so rushed. People around you may seem to rush your grief. They may begin to ask questions, such as where will you live, do you have insurance, are you going back to work, and will you remarry. STOP!! Answer those questions simply by stating, "I'm not ready to talk about that yet." While people may have concerns about your life, they cannot control how and at what pace you move forward. Protect your life and your grief. Be strong enough to tell others who seem intrusive that you'd rather not discuss a certain topic. Monitor your thinking to be consistent and realistic with where you are in your grieving process. Live in the now.

Reflection

Search your heart as you reflect on the questions.

Describe a time you felt joy in your life.

_____

_____

_____

_____

_____

Do you expect perfection from those who comfort you?

_____

_____

_____

_____

_____

Have you felt that you expect those who desire to help you to abandon their own responsibilities? If so, how do you resolve those feelings?

_____

_____

_____

_____

_____

Living with Grief

∾

"...A time to mourn and a time to dance."

Ecclesiastes 3:4

Embrace God as Your Father

Life's devastating times are too much for us to take on alone. God's hands are large enough to hold our hurts. There is power in the word of God. Recite the word of God in your mind, and let it become written on your heart. The word of God is life and provides joy and hope. He instructs us to "Fear Not" for He is with us.

His love is perfect for the times when you feel abandoned and alone, not to mention when you are full of doubts and questions of WHY? It's natural to have questions and want them answered. God knew the day your spouse was birthed that he would depart after his work was finished. He knows when we hurt, and if you experience a broken heart, God promises to heal it. He reminds us in Hebrews 13:5, *"Never will I leave you; never will I forsake you."* This peace and comfort are beyond anything else you'll ever experience in your life. Take Him at His word; allow Him to flood your mind and saturate your thoughts with indescribable love. If you can't pray, just say, "Jesus, I can't pray." Just say His name. Listen to worship music and allow yourself to be soothed by the words and melodies of the songs. Above all, trust in Him and in the people God sends to help you through your time of indescribable and unbearable pain.

Reflection

Search your heart as you reflect on the questions.

Since the death of your loved one, how has your belief in God changed?

_____

_____

_____

_____

_____

What thoughts of anxiety do you need to bring to God?

_____

_____

_____

_____

_____

How has your prayer life been altered?

_____

_____

_____

_____

_____

How do you pray?

- ❑ Conversation
- ❑ Listening
- ❑ Reading scripture
- ❑ Crying
- ❑ I can't pray. I just call His name, Jesus.

Do you still believe God answers prayers? If not, how can you begin to stir up the faith in your heart again?

_____

_____

_____

_____

_____

Set Boundaries with the Word NO

Today's society is interlaced with business, and we have become accustomed to being exhausted, leaving no time in our lives for rest and renewal. A yearly vacation is not enough. The notion that you will say no to someone is unthinkable in our fast-paced, technology-driven society. Oh, the looks, the soccer mom cliques, the gossip trails, the judgment—who can bear it? Well, the words "No" and "I'm not available" will be your new best friends as you navigate and restructure your very new reality.

Over-consumption of time for the wrong reasons in any area of your life can lead to unhealthy grief. Learning to create boundaries within your home, with family, with work, and in ministry is a gift to yourself and your family.

✿✿

Reflection

Search your heart as you reflect on the questions.

Write a grief letter or call those relatives you depend on. Describe what they can expect from you, your current feelings, and your needs; and state how they can support you during this time.

Make a list of who you need to contact.

_____

_____

_____

When death happens prematurely, people will ask questions and probe, causing you to relive the suffering or sudden surprise over and over and over again. It's important in the acceptance phase of grief to become accustomed to verbalizing who died in your life and how they died. I recall every introduction in my grief counselling circle amongst other widows and widowers. I said, "My name is Angela. I have a nine-year-old daughter. My husband died of a heart attack!" The more I said these words, the more comfortable I became with facing it as my new reality.

Some people will ask you to relive and recount each waking moment of that dreadful memory that is plastered in your mind. To protect my grief journey, I would simply say my rehearsed line. When they began to probe into personal details of how he died, if he was sick, how long he was sick, if his parents were living, and so on, there were times I was led to share full details. However, when I didn't desire sharing, I would say, "He lived a full life. Whether he died on the golf course or in the hospital, his date of death was predestined by God. And God knew this moment would occur and that I would need His unmatched love and peace."

Describe a time when you felt anxious about someone asking a question.

_____

_____

_____

_____

_____

What was your response?

_____

_____

_____

_____

_____

What has grief taught you about:

❑ Things that are important?

_____

_____

_____

❑ Yourself?

_____

_____

_____

❑ Your relationships?

_____

_____

_____

❑ Your faith?

_____

_____

_____

❑ Your treasures in heaven?

_____

_____

_____

❑ Your forgiveness toward yourself and others?

_____

_____

_____

❑ Your fears?

_____

_____

_____

Children Grieve, Too

It was essential to discuss grief with our daughter and let her know it was normal to cry or be sad and angry. I had to reassure her that I was present to help her through her pain. She was a member of a peer support group with other kids who lost a parent. Together, they participated in activities based on their level of understanding. One activity that I loved was when the leaders talked about a hole in their hearts. The kids broke a clay pot and had to try gluing it back together again. Well, they learned, no matter how hard you try, those pieces will never fit together as they once did; however, the pot could be put back together. The moral of the lesson is this: your heart will always have a piece missing from it, but you can learn to live despite the missing piece.

Reflection

Search your heart as you reflect on the questions.

Teach children that death is a part of life. Be honest about where the loved one is now and that they will not ever come home. Discuss ways that they would like to maintain traditions in the family. Let them see you grieve. Expressing feelings is important for growth.

Some activities you can do with young children:

❑ Draw a picture of your family.

- ❏ Have your children write about what they learned from your loved one who died.

- ❏ You and your child can write a good-bye letter.

- ❏ You and your children can decide how you will celebrate the loved one's birthday.

- ❏ Your child can make a superhero cape in honor of their parent.

- ❏ Have a moment of silence before special meals during the holiday season.

A Widow's Prayer

Jesus, my heart is broken, and I am hurting emotionally, exhausted physically, and weakened spiritually. My heart aches and moans. I pray from Ecclesiastes 3:11, *"He has made everything beautiful in its time; He has also set eternity in the human heart, yet no one can fathom what God has done from beginning to end."* God, no one but You in Your sovereign nature understands the mysteries of life. You hold them in eternity and reveal to us what You desire. I pray that the enemy will not use the natural circumstance of my husband's physical death to cause a spiritual death in me. I feel the spirit of depression. I feel withdrawn and detached from Your bosom. Draw me into Your comforting embrace.

God, let your peace rule over my raging thoughts. May Your love overcome my insecurities. May You become my husband and unmatched reassurance. May You be my constant provider and bless my home so that we lack in no area. I pray to have the patience of a planter in order to reap bountifully, as You open the windows of heaven and pour out uncontainable blessings. God, restore me as I rebuild my new life and find my new normal. God, surround me with an amazing support system that I can rely on. Endow me with Your wisdom.

Live in this scripture, recall it to God, stand on it, and meditate on it: *"Let the peace of Christ [the inner calm of one who walks daily with Him] rule in your hearts [deciding and settling questions that arise]; since as members of one body [of believers] you were called to peace. And be thankful [to God always]."* Colossians 3:15

In Jesus's name, Amen.

BIOGRAPHY

⤢

Angela Richardson Allen is motivated by helping and serving others. A native of Los Angeles, she went on to obtain a BA degree in Graphic Arts from San Diego State University and then an MBA from National University. Angela is the president and founder of Masterful Collective, which is a sports and event marketing boutique firm, and the Allen Insurance Agency. Angela has worked with professional athletes, the Off the Field Players' Wives Association, and Sam's Club on marketing endorsements and special events.

Angela was a devoted wife of nine years before suddenly losing her husband. As a widow, she is committed to helping other widows in their journey to continue to live. Angela is motivated by her desire to live life to the fullest, as she recognizes that life is short. Along with her daughter Amaya, she co-authored a picture book titled *A Place Far Away*, geared toward helping children cope with death and grief. Additionally, Angela has created a tool every family would benefit from called *The Ultimate Plan in a Box* to help families properly prepare for death. Follow them at www.angelaandamaya.com.